Rejoice and Be Glad

Daily Reflections for Easter to Pentecost 2024

D1559077

William Skudlarek, OSB

LITURGICAL PRESS

Collegeville, Minnesota

www.litpress.org

Nihil Obstat: Rev. Robert C. Harren, J.C.L., *Censor Librorum*
Imprimatur: ✝ Most Rev. Patrick M. Neary, C.S.C., Bishop of St. Cloud, May 9, 2023

Cover design by Monica Bokinskie. Cover art courtesy of Getty Images.

Scripture excerpts in this work are from the *Lectionary for Mass for Use in the Dioceses of the United States of America, second typical edition* © 2001, 1998, 1997, 1986, 1970 Confraternity of Christian Doctrine, Inc., Washington, DC. Used with permission. All rights reserved. No portion of this text may be reproduced by any means without permission in writing from the copyright owner.

Other Scripture texts in this work are taken from the *New American Bible, revised edition* © 2010, 1991, 1986, 1970 Confraternity of Christian Doctrine, Washington, DC, and are used by permission of the copyright owner. All Rights Reserved. No part of the New American Bible may be reproduced in any form without permission in writing from the copyright owner.

Where noted, Scripture quotations are from New Revised Standard Version Bible © 1989 National Council of the Churches of Christ in the United States of America. Used by permission. All rights reserved worldwide.

© 2023 by William Skudlarek, OSB
Published by Liturgical Press, Collegeville, Minnesota. All rights reserved. No part of this book may be used or reproduced in any manner whatsoever, except brief quotations in reviews, without written permission of Liturgical Press, Saint John's Abbey, PO Box 7500, Collegeville, MN 56321-7500. Printed in the United States of America.

ISSN: 2578-7004 (Print)
ISSN: 2578-7012 (Online)

ISBN: 978-0-8146-6819-1   978-0-8146-6820-7 (e-book)

Introduction

Much as we may insist that the fifty days of Easter are the high point of the Christian year, there is simply no getting around the fact that the spiritual life of most Catholics is focused on the forty days of Lent. Once Easter Sunday has come and gone, one can almost hear a collective sigh of relief. "I made it! Now we can get back to normal."

Making use of this little book of reflections, meditations, and prayers based on the Scripture texts for each day of the Easter season is a sign of your desire to reap and savor the fruits of your Lenten observance. With Easter, the emphasis shifts from what we do for the Lord through our Lenten prayer, fasting, and almsgiving, to what Jesus has done and continues to do in and for us through his passion, death, and resurrection, and through his presence in our lives and in all times and places: "And behold, I am with you always, until the end of the age" (Matt 28:20).

Our faith in the resurrection of Jesus from the dead is based on the testimony of those who knew and followed him prior to his crucifixion and then experienced his presence among them once more—occasionally appearing to them over a period of forty days (a significant number throughout Scripture) and powerfully thereafter through the outpouring of the Holy Spirit.

It is the Holy Spirit who keeps alive not only the memory but the very presence of the risen Christ in the lives of the baptized. It is the Holy Spirit who guides the church in developing ways of understanding and witnessing to Jesus Christ that make sense in our world today.

The Scripture texts for the celebration of the Eucharist during the fifty days of Easter are usually drawn from the Gospel of John and the Acts of the Apostles. John emphasizes that the risen Christ abides in those who believe in him—that is, in those who accept and trust him as the divine Word made flesh. The Acts of the Apostles tells us how the first generation of believers responded—sometimes well, sometimes not so well—to the challenge of proclaiming the transformative power of faith in Christ to both Jews and Gentiles, who populated the Roman Empire of the first century. The challenges we face may be different from theirs, but we have much to learn from the ways they met those challenges.

The prayer suggested for each day is often taken from the book of Psalms. These prayers of petition and thanksgiving, praise and lament, have served God's people for thousands of years. They still ring true today.

"We are an Easter People and Alleluia is our song!" Pope John Paul II spoke these words while on an apostolic visit to Australia, and then went on to say, "We are not looking for a shallow joy but rather a joy that comes from faith [and] grows through unselfish love." May these brief reflections help deepen and sustain your joy and unselfish love throughout these fifty days of Easter.

William Skudlarek, OSB

Reflections

Resurrection Running

Readings: Acts 10:34a, 37-43; Col 3:1-4 or 1 Cor 5:6b-8; John 20:1-9 or Mark 16:1-7

Scripture: [S]he ran . . . They both ran . . . (John 20:2, 4)

Reflection: There is a breathless quality about John's description of that first Easter morning. Mary of Magdala comes to the tomb when it is still dark, sees that it has been opened, and runs to tell Peter and the "disciple whom Jesus loved" that Jesus' body has been stolen. Peter and the Beloved Disciple come running to the tomb to see if it's true.

Running is a symbol of what has become of Jesus. When you walk, one foot is always touching the ground. When you run, there is a split second between each stride when both feet leave the earth and, for a moment at least, you are airborne. Those who run often and run well experience an incredible lightness of being, a spiritual élan, a "high" that is unmatched. The runner anticipates in a small and yet perfectly real way existence in a spiritual body, the kind of existence Jesus now possesses and that will be our next stage of life.

We experience this lightness of being, our share in the risen life of Christ, in those moments of our lives when prayer lifts us up, when we are spontaneously drawn to the side of someone in pain, when, in spite of what seem to be unending spirals of hatred and violence, we do not lose hope, confident that in the end good will triumph over evil through peaceful resistance, love, and forgiveness.

Christ is risen, *Alleluia!* He is truly risen, *Alleluia.* We share in his risen life, *Alleluia, alleluia, alleluia!*

Meditation: You may not be—or may no longer be—a runner, but if you are or were, you know the unique sense of joy that running can give—a joy that can be yours vicariously when you see a child who has just learned how to run. Reflect a bit on those moments and allow that reflection to shape your joyful response to the good news that "Christ is risen! He is risen indeed!"

Prayer: We hope in you, Lord.
Renew our strength that we may soar on eagles' wings.
May we run and not grow weary,
walk and not grow faint. (Based on Isa 40:31)

April 1: Monday within the Octave of Easter

Easter Mondays

Readings: Acts 2:14, 22-33; Matt 28:8-15

Scripture: "God raised this Jesus; of this we are all witnesses." (Acts 2:32)

Reflection: You may have heard about the workaholic who had a sign on his desk that read "Thank God it's Monday."

Some of us are probably thinking the same thing, but for the opposite reason. Thank God it's Monday and we finally have time to reflect on the incredibly tragic and incredibly glorious events we have commemorated and celebrated this past week.

Holy Week is an especially intense period of time in the church year for all of us. One can only imagine what it was like for those first followers of Jesus. It began with great excitement and hope, soon gave way to fear, confusion, horror, loss, and unspeakable grief. Then it exploded with the incredible realization that Jesus had been restored to life, but in a totally transformed and glorified form.

The disciples needed a lot of Mondays to begin to understand the meaning of what had taken place. Gradually it became clear. As Peter proclaimed to the crowd on Pentecost, God raised Jesus up, having freed him from death, because it was impossible for him to be held in its power.

We still need our Mondays to grasp that what is true for Jesus is also true for us. It is impossible for death to hold *us* in its power. Through faith and baptism, the risen Christ lives in us and we in Christ.

Meditation: It is certainly right and just to celebrate the resurrection of Jesus as God's victory over sin and death and as the promise of eternal life. It is also right and just to reflect on how the resurrection affects the way we live our lives. How would our lives be different if we did not believe that God raised Jesus and that he now lives in and among us? How does our belief in the resurrection affect the way we regard death—our own and that of others?

Prayer: Therefore my heart is glad, my soul rejoices;
           my body also dwells secure,
       For you will not abandon my soul to Sheol,
           nor let your devout one see the pit.
       You will show me the path to life,
           abounding joy in your presence,
           the delights at your right hand forever.
               (Ps 16:9-11)

A Job to Do

Readings: Acts 2:36-41; John 20:11-18

Scripture: Jesus said to her, "Mary!" (John 20:16)

Reflection: The Easter meeting of Jesus and Mary Magdalene is often portrayed as a scene of deep emotion and tender affection. "Mary," he says quietly; "Rabbouni" (My teacher), she replies, and then falls at his feet to embrace him.

That way of understanding the passage may be more in line with a sentimentalized portrayal of Easter than with what is actually found in the text of the Gospels.

The resurrection accounts are anything but sentimental. They are, in fact, rather hard and even frightening narratives, sprinkled throughout with words like "fear" and "awe" and "troubled." The risen Jesus inspires a sense of fright and wonder even in those who recognize him as the Jesus they knew, loved, and followed.

When Jesus says "Mary!" he might very well have been calling her to attention, much as an officer would to a soldier. Her "Rabbouni" then would have been something like the "Yes, sir!" of a new recruit to a drill sergeant.

When Mary embraces Jesus, he tells her to stop holding on to him. She has a job to do. "[G]o to my brothers and tell them, 'I am going to my Father and your Father, to my God and your God'" (John 20:17).

The resurrection stories are not about how nice it is to have Jesus back with us. Rather, they show us a risen and glorified Jesus Christ who empowers us to continue his mission.

The first to be so empowered, the first to understand and accept what the resurrection of Jesus is all about, the first to carry out his orders, is the Apostle of the Apostles, Mary of Magdala.

Thanks to her faith and courage, the church is off and running.

Meditation: Mary of Magdala shows us that it is natural to want to hold on to the one we love. But she also shows us that even though a loving attachment to Jesus may be what initially motivates us to do the work he calls us to, we may have to let go and move beyond the good feelings that come with that attachment if the work is to get done.

Prayer: I give you thanks, Lord Jesus, for the gift of your Holy Spirit who sustains my faith that you are with me at all times. When I do not feel your presence, help me to understand that you have not abandoned me but are entrusting me with your mission of bringing help and comfort to those in need.

Doing What Peter Did

Readings: Acts 3:1-10; Luke 24:13-35

Scripture: "[I]n the name of Jesus Christ the Nazorean, rise and walk." (Acts 3:6)

Reflection: The Italians have a delightful saying that goes, *"Se non è vero, è ben trovato,"* meaning, "Even if it's not true, it's well said."

A true story that may never have happened is about St. Charles Borromeo. In 1560 he was made a cardinal at the age of twenty-two by his uncle, Pope Pius IV, one of the popes of the powerful Medici family.

One day as the pope and his entourage were passing through the streets of Rome, a lame beggar approached, asking for alms. Summoning his nephew, the pope asked for the purse containing alms for the poor. He gave some coins to the beggar and then turned to his nephew and said, "Carlo, my son, is it not sad that the successor of Peter is not able to do as Peter did—to command this poor lame man to rise and walk in the name of Jesus Christ the Nazorean?"

"It is sad indeed," replied Charles Borromeo, "and the reason may very well be that the successor of Peter is not able to say, 'I have no silver or gold.'"

Perhaps we could apply a similar interpretation to the words of today's Gospel. Would it not be sad if our eyes were not opened, if we did not recognize the risen Jesus sharing his life with us in the breaking of the bread?

That would be sad indeed. And the reason might be that unlike the travelers to Emmaus, we may not be spending enough time with the Lord in prayer and meditation so that he can open the Scriptures to us.

Meditation: The Eucharist is not just about bread becoming the Body of Christ; it is about sacramentalized bread being broken and given, about bread being shared. Recognizing Jesus in the breaking of the bread means seeing Jesus in every act of sharing, especially when that sharing involves our being broken.

Prayer: I thank you, loving God, for the many gifts people have shared with me and for the many ways I have been able to share my life and my gifts with others. May I always be grateful for the many ways that sharing halves sorrow and doubles joy.

April 4: Thursday within the Octave of Easter

The Same but Not the Same

Readings: Acts 3:11-26; Luke 24:35-48

Scripture: "Have you anything here to eat?" (Luke 24:41)

Reflection: Resurrection does not mean resuscitation. If Jesus had been resuscitated, his disciples would recognize him when he appears to them, but they do not. They have to be convinced that it is really Jesus who is appearing to them. So he asks for a piece of baked fish and eats it in their presence.

Admittedly, the fact that the risen Jesus eats something suggests that he still has the same body he did before he died, in other words, that he has been resuscitated. But the question still remains: Why don't the disciples recognize him? He has not simply been restored but *transformed*. He is still the Jesus they knew, but he's Jesus in a completely different way. This is the work of resurrection, not resuscitation.

The apostle Paul tries to make sense of this "same but not the same" by speaking of a "spiritual body," which he contrasts with a "natural body" (1 Cor 15:44). However, that doesn't tell us what a spiritual body is like. We may think that it doesn't make any sense for someone who is now a spiritual body to be eating. However, if we're honest, we have to admit that we have no idea what a spiritual body is like, what it can or cannot do.

As Jesus eats a piece of fish, his disciples must have recalled the many times they shared meals with him, either by themselves or with sinners and tax collectors. Eating in their presence was the ideal way for Jesus to help them recognize him. This is the Jesus they have known all along, and yet they are beginning to learn how resurrection changes everything.

Meditation: Reflecting on the resurrection of Jesus may prompt thoughts about what it will mean for us to be raised from the dead. While we may not even begin to imagine what it will be like to be a "spiritual body," our faith in the resurrection of Jesus gives us hope that we too will be "the same but not the same" and that our joy will be complete.

Prayer: O LORD, our Lord,
                how awesome is your name through all the earth!
                You have made us little less than a god,
                crowned us with glory and honor.
                    (Paraphrase of Ps 8:2, 6)

April 5: Friday within the Octave of Easter

Extraordinarily Ordinary

Readings: Acts 4:1-12; John 21:1-14

Scripture: "Come, have breakfast." (John 21:12)

Reflection: In the 1999 Academy Award-winning film *American Beauty*, a high school beauty queen tells her friend that she plans to become a model. "There's nothing worse in life," she says, "than being ordinary."

What could be more ordinary than today's account of the appearance of the risen Jesus to seven of his disciples? It's just the opposite of what you would expect of someone who has risen from the dead and is now appearing to his followers. No blaring trumpets, no flashing lights, no "Hallelujah Chorus." Just someone on a lakeshore grilling fish for breakfast and telling his friends who have come home empty-handed that they might actually catch something if they drop their net off the other side of the boat.

We tend to think that we will only experience God in our lives by doing something extraordinary—spending long hours in prayer, going on a physically demanding pilgrimage, doing heroic acts of penance. But the usual way God becomes a real presence in our lives is through the ordinary activities of daily life. For those who believe in Jesus, these daily acts can be our response to the question Jesus puts to all of us: "Do you love me?" (John 21:17). When ordinary activities are done as an expression of love, they become extraordinary—and make us extraordinary as well.

As he told Peter, Jesus also tells us, "Feed my sheep" (John 21:17). Do ordinary things—make the bed, go to work, buy the groceries, take out the garbage, talk to your kids, visit your elderly parents. Show them how much you love them—and how much you love Jesus.

Meditation: Who among us does not pine for at least an occasional sense of being lifted above the ordinary by an unforgettable concert, a breathtaking view, falling head over heels in love? High points are important, but they do not and cannot last. What does last is joy in the ordinary good things of life that we can easily miss in our search for the extraordinary.

Prayer: The stone the builders rejected
            has become the cornerstone.
        By the Lord has this been done;
            it is wonderful in our eyes.
        This is the day the Lord has made;
            let us rejoice in it and be glad. (Ps 118:22-24)

Seeing Is Believing

Readings: Acts 4:13-21; Mark 16:9-15

Scripture: When they heard that he was alive and had been seen by her, they did not believe. (Mark 16:11)

Reflection: Easter hymns and prayers are filled with words like joy, glory, and triumph; the Gospel accounts, not so much. The words that stand out there are fear and doubt.

That is certainly true of Mark's account of the resurrection, which originally ended with the following verse: "Then they [Mary Magdalene, Mary the mother of James, and Salome] went out and fled from the tomb, seized with trembling and bewilderment. They said nothing to anyone, for they were afraid" (Mark 16:8).

An appendix was soon added to the Gospel so it would not end on such an abrupt and even disturbing note. Today's Gospel reading is that appendix (Mark 16:9-15).

However, the appendix is in its own way a surprising and sobering conclusion to Mark's account of the resurrection. It tells us that the primary response of the disciples of Jesus to his resurrection was skepticism. There are three references to their disbelief in this short passage: "they did not believe" (two times) and "they had not believed."

And yet, even as Jesus rebukes the eleven for their unbelief and hardness of heart, he sends them out to proclaim the good news to the whole of creation.

Perhaps he is telling them—and us, "Don't be surprised if what you say about me is rejected. Remember that you also did not believe those who saw me after I had risen. You had to see me for yourselves. That is why you cannot just speak about me to others. If you want others to believe in me, then let them see me—see my joy, see my compassion—in the way you live your lives."

Meditation: Faith in Jesus risen from the dead is more than believing the apostles' testimony that the Jesus who died on the cross appeared to them as living. Faith in the resurrection means witnessing to the presence and power of the risen Lord by the way you live. What is it about your life that shows people that Jesus is alive? What is still standing in the way?

Prayer: Lord Jesus, you have been glorified by the Father and are no longer bound by time and space. You now dwell in me and in all believers in every age. May we be ever eager to continue your mission, proclaiming that the kingdom of God is among us by what we joyfully say and do.

April 7: Second Sunday of Easter
(Sunday of Divine Mercy)

Touching Is Believing

Readings: Acts 4:32-35; 1 John 5:1-6; John 20:19-31

Scripture: "[B]ring your hand and put it into my side, and do not be unbelieving, but believe." (John 20:27)

Reflection: Believing, seeing, touching. They're all intertwined. "Seeing is believing" is true to a certain extent, but it has to be balanced by the reverse. If we do not believe, we will not see. Believing is what keeps us looking for something we are sure is there but can't see yet.

Where does touch come in? Thomas insists that he will only believe that it was the crucified and risen Jesus who appeared to the disciples if he sees the mark of the nails in Jesus' hands. Not only that—if he is to believe that the one his fellow disciples claim to have seen is actually the Lord, he must put his finger into the nailmarks and his hand into his side.

When Jesus appears to his disciples a week later, he tells Thomas to do exactly what Thomas said he would have to do if he was to believe—touch Jesus' pierced hands and side.

When Thomas utters his great profession of faith in Jesus as his Lord and God, Jesus replies, "Blessed are those who have not seen and have believed."

Notice that Jesus does not say, "Blessed are those who have not touched and have believed." Why not? Perhaps it is because those who come to believe—and continue to believe—in Jesus without seeing him are still invited to touch him. To touch him in the Eucharist and the other sacraments, yes, but also to touch him in the wounded people we see all around us.

Meditation: Touching is such an important element of Catholic worship and practice because in Jesus, God became flesh. As Pope Francis said, "Love is being able to take a hand that is dirty and the ability to look in the eyes of those who are in distress and say, 'For me, you are Jesus.'" Think of and give thanks for the many ways you have been touched by God and have been able to extend God's touch to others.

Prayer: As you have touched me, Lord, with mercy and forgiveness, comfort and healing, may I, with pure heart and mind, be ready to offer a loving touch to those who feel rejected and abandoned.

April 8: Annunciation of the Lord

God's Body Language

Readings: Isa 7:10-14; 8:10; Heb 10:4-10; Luke 1:26-38

Scripture: "[A] body you prepared for me." (Heb 10:5)

Reflection: Father Godfrey Diekmann, OSB, was a key figure in the Catholic liturgical reform that preceded and followed the Second Vatican Council. He was a dynamic speaker and teacher who didn't hesitate to be unconventional in getting his point across.

One day as he was visiting with guests at lunch, he became more and more animated. In a final outburst of enthusiasm, he pounded on the table and yelled, "It's not the resurrection, dang it! It's the incarnation!" (There are some who insist his expletive was a bit stronger.) In his typically dramatic way, Father Godfrey was insisting that God's becoming a human being, becoming a particular Palestinian Jew, is what sets Christianity apart from all other religious traditions. Other religions may speak of God appearing in human form, but only Christians believe that God actually became a particular human being.

The liturgical title of today's feast is the "Annunciation of the Lord." That title highlights Mary's willingness to accept becoming the mother of the Messiah. The feast might also be called "The Incarnation of the Lord." This emphasis on the incarnation would in no way deny the centrality of Mary's role, for it was from her body alone that the Son of God received the human body God had prepared for him.

Jesus of Nazareth, in whom God is incarnate, is God's body language. His words, his actions, his very physical being speak to us of God. To know what God is like, we have only to look at and listen to Jesus, who took flesh in Mary's womb and whose first lessons on what it means to be human came from her.

Meditation: Mary's response to the archangel Gabriel ("May it be done to me according to your word") shows us that God's will, even in something as stupendous as the incarnation, is normally accomplished through the willing participation of a human intermediary. Give thanks for the ways God's will has been and will be accomplished through you. Ask God to help you through the times when your own will gets in the way.

Prayer: "Sacrifice and offering you did not desire,
          but a body you prepared for me . . .
     Then I said, 'As is written of me in the scroll,
          Behold, I come to do your will, O God.' "
          (Heb 10:5, 7; cf. Ps 40:7-9)

Born and Reborn

Readings: Acts 4:32-37; John 3:7b-15

Scripture: "You must be born from above." (John 3:7)

Reflection: Buddhists speak of rebirth. What they mean is somewhat different from the popular notion of reincarnation. Catholics—well, Catholic liturgists, at least—speak of the day on which a saint died and on which their feast is celebrated as their *dies natalitia*, or birthday.

When Jesus tells Nicodemus that no one can see the kingdom of God without being born again (or, as our translation has it, being "born from above"; the Greek word has both meanings), he may be referring to the rebirth that will take place when we die and are raised to the fullness of life.

Catholics tend to interpret Jesus' words about being "born of water and Spirit" (John 3:5) as a direct reference to baptism. But perhaps Jesus is contrasting our natural birth with our heavenly birth. We are born of water, namely, of the amniotic fluid of the womb, when we come into this world. We are reborn of the Spirit when we are raised from the dead.

If this is true, then perhaps we should understand our baptism as a sign of the rebirth that awaits us when we pass from this life to the next. By our natural birth and by baptism, we are God's children now; what we will be has not yet been revealed.

In this life, we walk by faith, and not by sight. We believe that baptism is the promise of rebirth. We may not *feel* reborn, but the process has begun. The wind is blowing where it wills. The Spirit is at work preparing us for the fullness of life.

Meditation: Those of us who were baptized as infants obviously do not remember our baptisms. But if there are pictures or a video, or if our godparents or someone else who was there are still alive, we might be able to "create memories" of and then give thanks for this key moment in our lives.

Prayer: Lord God, loving Father, continue to strengthen the new life in Christ that I received in the waters of baptism. In this sacrament, you united me to your risen and glorified Son. May the grace of this sacrament fill my life with abundant joy, praise, and kindness.

Nobody Flees from Love

Readings: Acts 5:17-26; John 3:16-21

Scripture: For God did not send his Son into the world to condemn the world, but that the world might be saved through him. (John 3:17)

Reflection: In Brazil, an organization known as the "Association for Protecting and Assisting Convicts" runs prisons based on the vision of APAC's founder, Mario Ottoboni, who once said that criminals "are not dangerous people. They are only people who are not sufficiently loved."

One of the most remarkable features of the APAC facilities is that even though there are no guards, and some prisoners are actually entrusted with the keys to the prison, enabling them to come and go from the prison during scheduled hours, virtually no one tries to break out. An inmate who escaped from six prisons before entering APAC was asked why he did not attempt to escape anymore. *"Do amor ninguém foge,"* he replied. "Nobody flees from love."

In addition to learning a skill or craft, working, and studying, inmates or *recuperandos* (people who are recovering from their criminal acts), as they are called, are required to participate in counseling groups and religious services. They follow a twelve-step program and a strict daily schedule.

APAC prisons are committed to the principles of restorative justice (justice focused on healing and restoration rather than punishment), and its programs are shaped by the recognition that crime is the experience of rejection taken to its extreme. At APAC, rejection is countered by love. The presence of volunteers who freely choose to spend their time accompanying the inmates is essential to fostering this environment of love.

God sent his Son not to condemn the world but to love it. Who is more in need of love than those who have known rejection and whose crimes were a cry for help, for love, and ultimately, for God?

Meditation: Those most in need of love are often, if not always, those who are most difficult to love. Our faith that Jesus does not give up on us is ultimately what will keep us from giving up on others.

Prayer: [Y]ou, Lord, are a compassionate and gracious God,
            slow to anger, abounding in mercy and truth.
        Turn to me, be gracious to me;
            give your strength to your servant . . .
        Give me a sign of your favor:
            make my enemies see, to their confusion,
            that you, Lord, help and comfort me.
                (Ps 86:15-17)

An Angry God?

Readings: Acts 5:27-33; John 3:31-36

Scripture: [W]hoever disobeys the Son will not see life, but the wrath of God remains upon him. (John 3:36)

Reflection: What does Jesus mean when he says "the wrath of God remains" on those who disobey the Son? Does God actually get angry with sinners and punish them?

Attributing a disaster to the wrath of God almost always raises more questions than it answers. Some claimed Hurricane Katrina caused such terrible damage to New Orleans in 2005 because the city's immorality angered God. If that was the case, why was so little damage done to the French Quarter?

Whenever we apply human attributes, positive or negative, to God, we need to ask ourselves if Jesus manifested those attributes, for it is ultimately Jesus who reveals God to us.

There is a verse in the Gospels that specifically says Jesus did get angry—and it isn't in the account of the cleansing of the temple as we might expect. "Looking around at them with anger and grieved at their hardness of heart, he said to the man, 'Stretch out your hand'" (Mark 3:5). The anger of Jesus is a sign of his zeal, distress, exasperation, or, as Mark puts it, his grief when he confronts hardhearted hypocrisy. Jesus does not become angry because of an affront done to him, but because people are turning away from, or keeping others from, what is for their own good.

The wrath of God is actually God's grief over the suffering that sin (not God) inflicts on people.

"Righteous anger" is a phrase often used to describe indignation at injustice done to others. That may well be an understandable emotional response. However, striking out in anger will more often further harden the hearts of those who acted unjustly than soften them.

Meditation: When everything seems to be falling apart, and you're tempted to think it's because God is angry with you, it might be helpful to meditate on the words the prophet Hosea attributes to God: "I will not give vent to my blazing anger, / . . . For I am God and not a man, / the Holy One present among you; / I will not come in wrath" (11:9).

Prayer: Merciful and gracious is the LORD,
　　　　　　　slow to anger, abounding in mercy.
　　　　　　He will not always accuse,
　　　　　　　and nurses no lasting anger. (Ps 103:8-9)

April 12: Friday of the Second Week of Easter

Slow Down

Readings: Acts 5:34-42; John 6:1-15

Scripture: "For if this endeavor or this activity is of human origin, it will destroy itself. But if it comes from God, you will not be able to destroy them; you may even find yourselves fighting against God." (Acts 5:38-39)

Reflection: The Sanhedrin had arrested the apostles and put them in prison for proclaiming that Jesus was the promised Messiah who had been raised from the dead, but they escaped and continued their preaching. Arrested again, they were ordered to desist. They refused, brazenly defending themselves with the retort, "We must obey God rather than men" (Acts 5:29).

The members of the Sanhedrin were so infuriated by the impertinence of the apostles that they wanted them to be put to death. One of them, Gamaliel, the apostle Paul's teacher when he studied in Jerusalem (see Acts 22:3), intervened and advised caution. If what the apostles were doing was God's work, he argued, not only would they not be able to stop them, they would also be opposing God.

Commenting on Gamaliel's words, the Catholic biblical scholar Raymond Brown contended that while "it may not be true that every religious movement that is of human origin fails; nevertheless, the church would have been wiser many times in its history if it had used Gamaliel's principle to judge new developments in Christianity rather than reacting in a hostile manner too quickly."

What is true for the church in general is also true for us individually. While there are certainly movements and behaviors that are so patently wrong that they cannot be allowed to continue, in most cases a wait-and-see attitude would be the better response to new ideas and practices, even those that may infuriate us.

Meditation: It is sobering to think that we might be fighting against God if we oppose something that irritates us or that we think is at odds with what God asks of us. Deciding when to give space and time to something that doesn't seem right to us and when to say "Enough" requires discernment—the kind of discernment that demands prayer and good counsel.

Prayer: Lord, help me see that relationships are more important than who's right and who's wrong. If someone proposes an idea or speaks in a way that is truly not in accord with your will, show me how to say so without damaging our relationship.

Even Priests

Readings: Acts 6:1-7; John 6:16-21

Scripture: [E]ven a large group of priests were becoming obedient to the faith. (Acts 6:7)

Reflection: The peril of being a translator is cunningly conveyed in the Italian saying, *"Traduttore traditore"* (literally "Translator traitor"). Translations often betray the true meaning of the original text. Rarely, if ever, does a translation convey the exact connotation, emotion, and context that the original writer or speaker intended.

However, betrayal can also occur when a translation is too literal. For that reason, a translator often has to look for a "dynamic equivalent" of a word or phrase to convey its meaning more adequately in translation. Take, for example, the statement "even a large group of priests were becoming obedient to the faith." The word "even" is used here to translate the Greek particle *te*, which literally means "and." "And" is a neutral word, but "even" suggests surprise and admiration.

I'd be willing to bet that the original author of the Acts of the Apostles was indeed surprised that so many priests—who are usually presented in the Gospels as among the principal opponents of Jesus—were now his followers. For that reason, translating *"te"* in this passage as "and" would be a betrayal of the meaning and emotional content of his observation. The word "even" conveys the element of surprised admiration in a way that "and" does not.

For contemporary readers of this translation—especially readers who are ordained—that "even" could be the catalyst for serious reflection. "Even" priests have to make time to "devote [themselves] to prayer and to the ministry of the word" (Acts 6:4) if they are to be faithful preachers and teachers and find joy in their ministry.

Meditation: The word "even" can also lead us to reflect on the utter gratuity of the love God shows us in Christ Jesus. It's freely given even when we don't deserve it. Scripture puts it this way: "But God, who is rich in mercy, because of the great love he had for us, even when we were dead in our transgressions, brought us to life with Christ" (Eph 2:4-5).

Prayer: Even me, Lord, even me. . . . Even when I fall back into a bad habit I am striving to overcome, you forgive me and encourage me to keep on trying. Even when I forget you, you do not forget me. Even though I am not worthy to receive you under my roof, you continue to nourish me with your Body and Blood. Even me, Lord, even me.

April 14: Third Sunday of Easter

Changing Hearts and Minds

Readings: Acts 3:13-15, 17-19; 1 John 2:1-5a; Luke 24:35-48

Scripture: Then he opened their minds to understand the Scriptures. (Luke 24:45)

Reflection: A friend told me about a social media post he read that claimed, "People change their minds when you show them facts." He responded to that post saying, "Actually, studies show that's not true," and provided links to three studies. The poster replied, "Yeah, well, I still think it's true."

Like many of their contemporaries, the disciples had made up their minds that the Messiah would be a conquering hero who would free Israel and inaugurate a reign of peace and prosperity. Jesus needed to show them that it was through suffering, death, and resurrection that the Messiah would bring salvation, and that forgiveness of sins, preached in his name, would not be for the people of Israel only, but for all nations.

To change their minds, "facts" were not enough. He himself, standing in front of them, eating a piece of baked fish, was a fact. However, the disciples were so overwhelmed that they were still not convinced that their crucified teacher, now apparently risen from the dead, was the promised Messiah.

To help them understand the kind of Messiah he was, Jesus undoubtedly pointed to the passages in which Isaiah spoke of a "suffering servant," one who would bear "the punishment that makes us whole" (Isa 53:5), one whom God would send to be "a light to the nations, / that my salvation may reach to the ends of the earth" (Isa 49:6).

It took time, but gradually the disciples did change their minds and tirelessly proclaimed the good news of God's boundless love for us, shown in the life, passion, death, and resurrection of Jesus of Nazareth.

Meditation: The life of a Christian is one of constant conversion. We are continually being called to a change of mind and heart, to a greater understanding of who Jesus is and of the limitless extent of God's love for us and all people. Have there been times when you have had to change your mind about Jesus or the church in some way? What helped you do that?

Prayer: In the LORD I trust;
> I do not falter.
> Examine me, Lord, and test me;
>> search my heart and mind.
> Your mercy is before my eyes;
>> I walk guided by your faithfulness. (Ps 26:1-3)

April 15: Monday of the Third Week of Easter

Faith: A Good Work?

Readings: Acts 6:8-15; John 6:22-29

Scripture: "This is the work of God, that you believe in the one he sent." (John 6:29)

Reflection: When people disagree, they are rarely motivated to come to a deeper understanding of the issue they are disagreeing about. Rather, it's all about winning an argument and proving someone wrong.

So it was in the sixteenth century. Martin Luther and other reformers were dismayed by church practices—the selling of indulgences being a main one—that were grounded in the belief that we have to "earn" our salvation. The reformers insisted that we are saved by faith alone (*sola fide*) and cited the letter to the Ephesians: "For by grace you have been saved through faith, and this is not from you; it is the gift of God; it is not from works, so no one may boast" (2:8-9).

In defense of the importance of good works, Catholics cited the letter of James: "What good is it, my brothers, if someone says he has faith but does not have works? Can that faith save him?" (2:14).

Neither party, it seems, bothered to ask some basic questions: What is faith? Can faith be misdirected? What are works? Why are they done? Or, with reference to today's Gospel reading, what is the "work of God" we are called to?

As recorded in the Gospel of John, for Jesus, the "work of God" means having faith in the one God has sent. The "good work" we are called to do is believing, trusting in God's love for us even though we do not deserve it, and then putting that love into practice.

As is so often the case, what seems like either/or may actually be both/and. It all depends on how we understand what we are disagreeing about. This level of understanding requires good will, honest listening, and serious effort, but the richness it brings to our lives is well worth it.

Meditation: "To believe" means a lot more than having correct ideas about someone or something. It means believing in someone, giving ourselves to another person in a relationship of unconditional trust. To grow in that kind of faith, we would do well to make our own the prayer of the fourteenth-century English mystic Julian of Norwich:

Prayer: "All shall be well, and all shall be well, and all manner of things shall be well."

Becoming Bread

Readings: Acts 7:51–8:1a; John 6:30-35

Scripture: "I am the bread of life . . ." (John 6:35)

Reflection: When we speak of the Eucharist, it can be difficult to explain how bread and wine are changed into the Body and Blood of Christ but still look and taste like bread and wine.

In an effort to explain this difficult concept, medieval theologians used categories of ancient Greek philosophy to develop the doctrine of transubstantiation. Transubstantiation means that what changes (the "trans" part of "transubstantiation") is the *substance*—the essence—of bread and wine. What remains, what is not changed, is what is often referred to as the *accidents* of bread and wine—their appearance and taste.

Another way of understanding the mystery of the Eucharist can be found in an expression I heard when I lived in Brazil: "*Ó Jesus sacramentado,*" meaning "O sacramented Jesus."

For the widow I was visiting, that delightful exclamation was more or less the equivalent of "O my God." What it suggested to me, however, was another way of understanding the eucharistic mystery of the Real Presence of Jesus under the signs of bread and wine. In the celebration of the Eucharist, Jesus is *sacramented*, that is, *he becomes* the sacramental sign of bread and wine. This understanding complements the traditional notion that bread and wine are *transubstanti-ated*, that is, *they become* the Body and Blood of Jesus Christ.

Jesus refers to himself as "the living bread that came down from heaven" (John 6:51). In becoming the bread and the wine of the Eucharist, Jesus offers us the preeminent sign of his body given for us, his blood poured out for us. In becoming bread and wine for us, he manifests his desire to remain in us, to nourish our hunger and thirst for God.

Meditation: Popular Catholic attempts to explain the Eucharist run the gamut from gross cannibalism ("That's real flesh and blood that I am consuming") to shallow representation ("It's just a symbol"). How might our appreciation of the Eucharist be increased if we were to speak of Jesus becoming bread and wine for us in the Eucharist?

Prayer: Praise and thanks to you, Lord Jesus Christ, who in this sacrament of bread and wine, offer yourself to us as nourishment for everlasting life.

A Hounding God

Readings: Acts 8:1b-8; John 6:35-40

Scripture: "And this is the will of the one who sent me, that I should not lose anything of what he gave me . . ." (John 6:39)

Reflection: The poem "The Hound of Heaven" beautifully and movingly expresses Jesus' words that God does not want him to lose any of those who have been entrusted to him. To put it in more contemporary language, Jesus never gives up on us, no matter what. He continues to "hound" us.

Like much poetry from the Victorian period, however, modern readers can be turned off by language that is all but unintelligible. What are we to make of such lines as "Ah! must Thou char the wood ere Thou canst limn with it?"

The author of "The Hound of Heaven" was the mid-nineteenth-century English Roman Catholic Francis Thompson (1859–1907). He abandoned his medical studies to pursue his talent as a writer and poet. His health was always frail and then further deteriorated because of his addiction to opium, which he had begun taking for a nervous condition. He died at the age of forty-seven of tuberculosis. His poem is almost certainly autobiographical, expressing his attempts to put God out of his life and his realization that God is not so easily dismissed.

One of the reasons Thompson was so adamant about not wanting God in his life was his fear that "having Him, I must have naught beside."

Thompson responds to that fear in the closing lines of his poem, recognizing that if we drive God away, we drive love away as well:

> Ah, fondest, blindest, weakest
> I am He Whom thou seekest!
> Thou dravest love from thee, who dravest me.

Meditation: Times of great disappointment or intense physical or emotional suffering are often made even worse by the sense that God has abandoned us and doesn't care about us. What if we thought of God not so much as a "fixer," but as one who shares our suffering, who is constantly seeking us out to be at our side, consoling and encouraging us?

Prayer: Where can I go from your spirit?
>   From your presence, where can I flee?
> If I ascend to the heavens, you are there;
>   if I lie down in Sheol, there you are.
> If I take the wings of dawn
>   and dwell beyond the sea,
> Even there your hand guides me,
>   your right hand holds me fast. (Ps 139:7-10)

The Gift of Baptism

Readings: Acts 8:26-40; John 6:44-51

Scripture: "What is to prevent my being baptized?" (Acts 8:36)

Reflection: Baptism is the Easter sacrament par excellence. An especially meaningful way for Catholics to celebrate Easter is by participating in an Easter Vigil service at which adult catechumens profess their faith in the Father, Son, and Holy Spirit, are drenched with or plunged into the cleansing and life-giving waters of baptism, and are anointed with the chrism of confirmation. Then, together with the Christian community that surrounds, affirms, and supports them, they are nourished with the Body and Blood of Christ in the Eucharist, the sign of our communion with God and one another. By participating in this awe-inspiring celebration, our own baptisms are renewed.

Adult baptism emphasizes and expresses a personal decision for Christ and his church. Infant baptism expresses the gratuity of God's offer of new life in Christ. We don't earn it; we don't merit it; we receive it as pure gift. The Ethiopian eunuch asked, "What is to prevent my being baptized?" Our question might be, "What is to prevent God from offering the grace of life in Christ to a child?"

The Easter renewal of our baptism invites us to give thanks for the gift of new life in Christ that was given to most of us when we were baptized as infants. In giving thanks for our baptism, we give thanks for the community of incredible men and women, past and present, that we are now a part of. By their lives of prayer, acts of service, and their artistic and intellectual gifts, they have contributed to the New Creation inaugurated by Jesus Christ, in whom the church beholds the face of God.

Meditation: If you were baptized as an infant, you may have photographs or even a video of the ceremony. Take a look at them and see the joy in the faces of those who welcomed you into the community of believers. What joy has your baptism brought you? What joy are you longing for?

Prayer: How precious is your mercy, O God!
        The children of Adam take refuge in the
            shadow of your wings.
        They feast on the rich food of your house;
            from your delightful stream you give them
            drink.
        For with you is the fountain of life,
            and in your light we see light. (Ps 36:8-10)

Just a Symbol?

Readings: Acts 9:1-20; John 6:52-59

Scripture: "[U]nless you eat the Flesh of the Son of Man and drink his Blood, you do not have life within you." (John 6:53)

Reflection: When the crowd says that all of Jesus' talk about eating his flesh and drinking his blood is unacceptable, Jesus doesn't back down. But he does go on to say that "the flesh is of no avail" and that his words are "spirit and life" (John 6:61).

In other words, when Jesus says that eating the flesh and drinking the blood of the Son of Man is how we remain in him, he is not talking about cannibalism. Rather, by using strong and indeed shocking words, he insists that it is in and through his full and now risen humanity, his glorified flesh and blood, that God offers us the fullness of life.

This passage is often used to prove that the Eucharist is *really* the Body and Blood of Christ and not just a symbol. But symbols are not merely signs pointing to something real; symbols can contain the reality itself.

It might help to remember another symbol that Jesus uses to speak of our need to be united with him in order to share in his divine life: "I am the vine, you are the branches. Whoever remains in me and I in him will bear much fruit . . ." (John 15:5). When we hear those words, we don't ask, "How can Jesus be a vine? How can we be branches?" We know Jesus is using symbolic language and we have no doubt about the full meaning of these symbols.

To understand Jesus' words about eating his flesh and drinking his blood as symbolic language does not in any way deny the Real Presence of Christ in these sacramental signs. We believe he is really and truly present there, even though we may struggle to find adequate words to fully express our faith.

Meditation: A national flag is one example of what it means to be more than just a symbol. Any sign of contempt for the flag arouses anger and concern because it is seen as an expression of disrespect for the people it stands for. When we think about the Eucharist as the highest expression of that kind of symbol, we can easily see that it doesn't just point to Christ; it is the very presence of Christ.

Prayer: Jesus, when I look upon you veiled in this sacrament, I ardently pray that one day I may see your face and be blessed with the vision of your glory. (St. Thomas Aquinas, from the hymn *Adoro te devote*)

Build It, and They Will Come

Readings: Acts 9:31-42; John 6:60-69

Scripture: The Church throughout all Judea, Galilee, and Samaria was at peace. [It] was being built up and walked in the fear of the Lord, and with the consolation of the Holy Spirit [it] grew in numbers. (Acts 9:31)

Reflection: "If you build it, they will come" is one of the most memorable—but misquoted—lines from the movies. It comes from *Field of Dreams*, a 1989 film about an Iowa farmer who builds a baseball diamond in his cornfield, having heard a voice telling him: "If you build it, he will come."

When Luke says that the church was "being built up" and that it "grew in numbers," one can only wonder if there might be some truth to the saying, "If you build it, they will come."

Of course, Luke is not referring to the construction of a building but to the growth of the community of believers in wisdom, love, and piety. Luke makes this clear when he says believers "walked in the fear of the Lord," meaning that they continued to be filled with awe and wonder that the Jesus they may have personally known had been raised from the dead and exalted at God's right hand.

Add to that their experience of the "consolation of the Holy Spirit," and one is not surprised to learn that this little flock of believers grew in numbers.

What people especially noticed about the early followers of Jesus was that their fervent devotion to God and their care and concern for people in need was building them into a community marked by fraternal love and consolation.

They noticed, and they came.

Meditation: If we consciously attended to the "building up" of our parishes and religious communities, making them vibrant centers of worship where the faithful offer praise and thanksgiving to God and where they are equipped to love one another, care for the poor, and work for social justice, might more people begin to think that being part of a Christian community is something worth investigating?

Prayer: Unless the LORD build the house,
        they labor in vain who build.
    Unless the LORD guard the city,
        in vain does the guard keep watch.
    It is vain for you to rise early
        and put off your rest at night,
    To eat bread earned by hard toil—
        all this God gives to his beloved in sleep.
        (Ps 127:1-2)

April 21: Fourth Sunday of Easter

No Other Name?

Readings: Acts 4:8-12; 1 John 3:1-2; John 10:11-18

Scripture: "There is no salvation through anyone else . . ." (Acts 4:12)

Reflection: Peter's words have sometimes been interpreted to mean that if you don't believe that Jesus is the incarnate Son of God who died for our sins and rose from the dead, you have no hope of being saved.

But Peter's immediate concern is not about who is going to heaven. Rather, he is insisting that it was God acting through Jesus Christ the Nazorean, who cured (saved) the lame man—not Peter or anyone else.

But what about Peter's statement that there is "no salvation through anyone else"? Doesn't that imply that salvation is only for those who believe in Jesus?

Maybe that is what Peter believed at the time. But if so, he changed his mind.

Sometime later, when he was a guest at the house of Simon the tanner in Joppa, Peter had a vision of a large sheet filled with unclean animals and heard a voice telling him: "Slaughter and eat." He resisted, and then heard a voice saying, "What God has made clean, you are not to call profane" (Acts 10:11-15).

Peter was then invited to the house of Cornelius, a Roman centurion who lived in Caesarea. Cornelius, a Gentile, told Peter about his vision of a man in dazzling robes who stood before him and said, "Cornelius, your prayer has been heard and your almsgiving remembered before God." Peter then understood that "God shows no partiality" and that "in every nation whoever fears him and acts uprightly is acceptable to him" (Acts 10:31, 34-35).

In and through Jesus, God graciously offers healing and life to all people, even those who may never have heard of him.

Meditation: Can we, like Peter, recognize the Spirit of God at work outside the boundaries of the church in ways that are new to us? Or do we tend to judge others as in error if they think, act, or believe in a way that is different from our own?

Prayer: May the nations be glad and rejoice;
for you judge the peoples with fairness,
you guide the nations upon the earth.
May the peoples praise you, God;
may all the peoples praise you! (Ps 67:5-6)

A Gate, Not a Gatekeeper

Readings: Acts 11:1-18; John 10:1-10

Scripture: "I am the gate for the sheep." (John 10:7)

Reflection: If Jesus had said, "I am the gate for God," we'd probably have a fairly good idea of what he meant. God comes to us through the gate that is Jesus, and, as we so often pray, we go to God "through Jesus Christ our Lord."

However, what Jesus says is "I am the gate for the sheep." The meaning of that metaphor is less clear. In fact, the evangelist John tells us that "[a]lthough Jesus used this figure of speech, they did not realize what he was trying to tell them" (10:6).

A passage in a novel by the Canadian writer Louise Penny suggests one way of understanding what it means to enter the sheepfold through the gate that is Jesus. She writes, "It is so easy to get mired in the all too obvious cruelty of the world. It's natural. But to really heal, we need to recognize the goodness too." Entering the sheepfold though the gate that is Jesus means approaching others with a willingness to recognize their goodness rather than with an eagerness to pass judgment on them for their faults.

He who said "I am the gate for the sheep" also said "And if anyone hears my words and does not observe them, I do not condemn him, for I did not come to condemn the world but to save the world" (John 12:47).

Jesus saves people, makes them whole, not by judging them but by loving them, forgiving their failures, and thus making it possible for them to change. He calls us to share in that saving mission by doing the same.

Meditation: What are the immoral behaviors or annoying traits of others that we tend to get especially "mired in," as Louise Penny puts it? Could it be that the reason we are so irritated by particular behaviors and traits is that they're like our own? What practical steps can we take to approach others—and ourselves—through the gate that is Jesus?

Prayer: Be a gate for me, Lord Jesus. A gate to patience, forgiveness, compassion, love, and joy.

Tarsus Time

Readings: Acts 11:19-26; John 10:22-30

Scripture: Then [Barnabas] went to Tarsus to look for Saul . . . (Acts 11:25)

Reflection: Saul's return to his hometown of Tarsus must have been painful. After his dramatic conversion on the way to Damascus, he began proclaiming Jesus as the Messiah. However, he ran into such opposition that "the brothers . . . took him down to Caesarea and sent him on his way to Tarsus" (Acts 9:30).

During the years he spent back in Tarsus, Saul probably spent a lot of time wondering what went wrong. Why did he provoke such opposition when he called others to accept Jesus as the Messiah? He must also have given a lot of time to prayer and meditation and thought about how he would do things differently if the apostles should ever again ask for his help.

And then Barnabas showed up and asked Paul to join him in Antioch where there was a rupture between Jewish and Gentile believers.

Saul needed those long years in Tarsus to realize who he was and to recognize that overcoming the division between Jews and Gentiles was at the very heart of the Good News. Furthermore—and this was Paul's great new insight—we do not have to amass good works to live fully and forever. We only need to open our hearts to the love and mercy that God freely offers us and then let that divine love and mercy flow through us to others.

Sometimes it is only after falling flat on our faces and being sent back home that we begin to recognize how absolutely essential it is to spend time in prayer, sacred reading, and meditation. Such "Tarsus time" allows us to set aside our own agendas and be ready to welcome a Barnabas—someone who believes in us and shows us the way forward—into our lives.

Meditation: Think back on the times you have failed (and we all have) despite your best efforts and good intentions. What has helped you regain confidence in yourself? Could it have involved becoming more confident that the risen Christ dwells within you?

Prayer: Though my flesh and my heart fail,
            God is the rock of my heart, my portion forever.
                (Ps 73:26)

Light in the Darkness

Readings: Acts 12:24–13:5a; John 12:44-50

Scripture: "I came into the world as light, so that everyone who believes in me might not remain in darkness." (John 12:46)

Reflection: Once, when I was a young teenager, I woke up in the middle of the night to find myself sitting on the floor. I realized that I must have been sleepwalking, so I got up to make my way back to my bed. The room was pitch black, and after a few steps, I stumbled into a piece of furniture. At that point, I was totally disoriented, not sure if I was in my own room or some other part of the house, afraid to move lest I fall and hurt myself. All I could do was sit on the floor and call for help. My mother heard me, came upstairs, and turned on the light. I could now see that I was, in fact, still in my own room and could go back to bed without fear of stumbling on something or falling down the stairs.

That simple but at the time scary experience taught me something about the scriptural image of light that is so often used of God, Jesus, and the law.

In a certain sense, light doesn't change anything. Rather, it allows us to see what had been shrouded in darkness and to change what needs to be changed—which may be ourselves and our way of looking at things rather than something outside of ourselves that we want God to make better or take away.

So often our prayers express our hope that God will change something. Maybe God is not so much into changing things but rather providing the light that makes it possible for us to see what can and should be changed and how *we* might be able to do the changing.

Meditation: Have you ever had one of those "Aha!" moments when you see things in a new light? How did that light change you? And what were you able to change when you saw things differently?

Prayer: The LORD is my light and my salvation;
                     whom should I fear?
             The LORD is my life's refuge;
                     of whom should I be afraid? (Ps 27:1)

April 25: Saint Mark

They Were Afraid

Readings: 1 Pet 5:5b-14; Mark 16:15-20

Scripture: The chosen one at Babylon sends you greeting, as does Mark, my son. (1 Pet 5:13)

Reflection: Writing from Rome ("Babylon"), Peter refers to Mark as "my son." The Acts of the Apostles speaks of a "John who is called Mark" who accompanied Barnabas and Saul on a relief mission to Jerusalem (12:12). Is that who wrote the Gospel of Mark? Maybe, but we can't be sure.

The Gospel of Mark, now generally regarded as the first of the four Gospels, was probably written to encourage Christians to remain firm in their faith in Jesus, the Son whom God sent to rescue humanity by his ministry of teaching and healing and, above all, by his passion and death on a cross.

Mark ends his Gospel by saying that when an angel told the women who came to the tomb that Jesus had been raised, they "went out and fled from the tomb, seized with trembling and bewilderment. They said nothing to anyone, for they were afraid" (16:8).

An appendix was later added to Mark's Gospel by those who felt that his ending was too abrupt. Ironically, that appendix, probably not written by Mark, is what we hear on his feast day.

The resurrection of Jesus is indeed reason for us to rejoice. But what if you were with those women who came to the tomb that morning to anoint the body of Jesus, still shaken and sorrowing because of his horrible death on a cross? Wouldn't you wonder just what was going on and how this was going to change your life? Might you too have been afraid?

Meditation: We instinctively shrink from suffering of any kind, and yet one of Mark's main concerns in writing his Gospel is that Jesus saves us through his suffering; he had to suffer. Suffering is the necessary preamble to resurrection. Can you see evidence in your own life or the lives of others that this is true?

Prayer: My God, my God, why have you abandoned me?
Why so far from my call for help,
from my cries of anguish?
My God, I call by day, but you do not answer;
by night, but I have no relief.
Yet you are enthroned as the Holy One;
you are the glory of Israel.
In you our fathers trusted;
they trusted and you rescued them.
(Ps 22:2-5)

The Way of Jesus

Readings: Acts 13:26-33; John 14:1-6

Scripture: "I am the way and the truth and the life." (John 14:6)

Reflection: The "Declaration on the Relation of the Church to Non-Christian Religions" is the shortest and yet one of the most important documents of the Second Vatican Council (1962–65). It calls on Catholics to "recognize, preserve and promote the good things, spiritual and moral," of other religious traditions (*Nostra Aetate*, 2).

That summons might give the impression that the council was underplaying Jesus referring to himself as "the way and the truth and the life" and commissioning the eleven to "make disciples of all nations" (Matt 28:19).

When Jesus refers to himself as the way, the truth, and the life, he means that his way of self-giving and inclusive love reveals God's way and is the way we are to live. Dying to self is the true way that gives life.

Jesus teaches: "For whoever wishes to save his life will lose it, but whoever loses his life for my sake will find it" (Matt 16:25). This is the way Jesus lives: he associates with tax collectors and sinners, cures the servant of a Roman centurion and the daughter of a Syrophoenician woman, reveals himself as the Messiah to a Samaritan woman.

The more we get to know devout followers of other religious traditions, the more we see that the way of self-giving service is not exclusive to Christians. We can indeed see, be inspired by, and give thanks for the spiritual and moral riches found outside the church. They show that "the spirit of the LORD fills the world" (Wis 1:7).

If you ask God to show you the way, be ready for God to open your eyes to the divine way manifested not only in our saints but in those of other religious traditions as well.

Meditation: Countless men and women have been inspired by the example of such people as Gandhi (Hindu), Thich Nhat Hanh (Buddhist), and Rumi (Muslim). Are there people of other religious traditions whose lives have helped you appreciate and follow the way of Jesus?

Prayer: Make known to me your ways, LORD;
              teach me your paths.
          Guide me by your fidelity and teach me,
              for you are God my savior,
              for you I wait all the day long. (Ps 25:4-5)

April 27: Saturday of the Fourth Week of Easter

The Language God Speaks

Readings: Acts 13:44-52; John 14:7-14

Scripture: "Whoever has seen me has seen the Father." (John 14:9)

Reflection: Even though God told Moses, "[Y]ou cannot see my face, for no one can see me and live" (Exod 33:20), we long for a God we can see. At the Last Supper, when the apostle Philip pleaded with Jesus, "Master, show us the Father, and that will be enough for us," Jesus told him, "Whoever has seen me has seen the Father" (John 14:8-9).

Jesus is God's response to this deep yearning for a God who can be seen, heard, touched. In Jesus, God becomes incarnate, takes on human flesh. The "Utterly Other" becomes one of us.

One way of expressing the great mystery of the incarnation is to see Jesus as God's "body language." In his body Jesus shows God's closeness to us when he touches lepers, the blind, the lame, and the deaf to cure them; hugs children; enjoys food and drink—to such an extent that his enemies defamed him as a glutton and a drunkard (Matt 11:19). The physicalness of Jesus is emphasized by the Greek word *splagchnizomai*, which is used throughout the Gospels to describe Jesus (and, interestingly, two characters in Jesus' parables: the father of the prodigal son and the master who

60   *Saturday of the Fourth Week of Easter*

forgave a large debt; Luke 15:20; Matt 18:27). It is usually translated as feeling pity or having compassion. What it literally means is that Jesus is so deeply moved by human suffering that he feels it in the pit of his stomach.

Words convey ideas, but our bodies communicate even more. They express who we are, what we're feeling, even what we're thinking. A smile, a frown, a slouch, what we do with our hands and our eyes—all these bodily gestures either reinforce or weaken what we say. If my words say one thing, but my body communicates something else, people will instinctively know which to believe.

Jesus reveals God as a loving, compassionate Father. His bodily actions make real the truth of his words, as do ours.

Meditation: How do I experience my body? Fretting about my appearance? Worried about it because of age or illness? Don't really think about it that much? Have I ever experienced gratitude for all that I can give and receive because of my body?

Prayer: You formed my inmost being;
            you knit me in my mother's womb.
        I praise you, because I am wonderfully made;
            wonderful are your works! (Ps 139:13-14)

Remaining in Jesus

Readings: Acts 9:26-31; 1 John 3:18-24; John 15:1-8

Scripture: "Remain in me, as I remain in you." (John 15:4)

Reflection: In his Gospel, the evangelist Mark says that Jesus "went up the mountain and summoned those whom he wanted and they came to him. He appointed twelve [whom he also named apostles] that they might be with him and he might send them forth to preach" (Mark 3:13-14).

The parallel passages in the other two Synoptic Gospels leave out the phrase "that they might be with him," mentioning only that Jesus chose twelve and sent them out to preach.

Could that omission be the reason the evangelist John put so much emphasis on remaining with Jesus when he wrote his Gospel? Could it be that already in the earliest days of the church, ministers of the Gospel, the Good News of Jesus Christ, had become so focused on evangelizing and adding to the number of believers that they were losing sight of the need to remain with Jesus in prayer and meditation, with the result that the church was splitting up into factions and ministry was turning into clericalism?

No matter how much good work preachers and other church ministers have done or wish to do, unless they remain in Christ, remain faithful to prayer and meditation, they run a double risk. If they think their ministry has been a success, they risk becoming petty tyrants in their own small kingdoms. And if things do not turn out the way they think they should, they risk becoming disgruntled cynics.

Jesus calls all of us to bear much fruit and become his disciples. We can only do that if we accept and relish his invitation to be with him, to remain in him.

Meditation: "Remaining with Jesus" is true prayer. Don't worry about impressing him with pious words or thoughts. Just be present to Jesus and let Jesus be present to you. That might seem like a waste of time, but think of how good it is simply to be with someone you love.

Prayer: My home is by your altars,
               Lord of hosts, my king and my God!
            Blessed are those who dwell in your house!
               They never cease to praise you. (Ps 84:4-5)

April 29: Saint Catherine of Siena

What Are We Forgetting?

Readings: Acts 14:5-18; John 14:21-26

Scripture: "The Advocate, the Holy Spirit whom the Father will send in my name—he will teach you everything and remind you of all that I told you." (John 14:26)

Reflection: When Jesus tells his disciples that the Father will send the Holy Spirit to remind them of all that he told them, he is presuming that there are things his followers will forget. In fact, over the centuries there were a good many things the church forgot. The Holy Spirit had a lot of reminding to do—and still does.

Think, for example, of the sixteenth century when the Holy Spirit had to remind the church that God's favor was freely given and did not have to be earned by doing good works.

What might the Holy Spirit be reminding the church today about all that Jesus told us, both by word and by example? Three areas would seem to stand out:

Jesus' insistence that the poor have a place of honor in the kingdom and that wealth can all too easily keep us out (Mark 10:23; Luke 6:20);

Jesus' refusal to abide by social standards and expectations that marginalize women because of *a priori* notions of what they can and cannot do, demonstrated, for example, by sending Mary Magdalene to be the "Apostle to the Apostles" with news of his resurrection (John 20:17-18);

Jesus' praise of individuals who did not belong to the chosen people or were not his followers but whose lives manifested compassion and faith. Think, for example, of the Samaritan woman at the well (John 4:4-26), the insistent Syrophoenician woman (Mark 7:24-30), and the compassionate Roman centurion (Matt 8:5-13).

Nor should we forget Jesus' response to John's attempt to prevent someone who was not part of their company from casting out demons in Jesus' name. Jesus said to him, "Do not prevent him, for whoever is not against you is for you" (Luke 9:50).

Meditation: Think of a book, film, conversation, or a passing remark or encounter that reminded you of what Jesus taught us but which we all too often "forget" or ignore. The Holy Spirit often uses such means to get our attention and prod us to action.

Prayer: What am I forgetting, Lord Jesus? Why do I not remember that one of your most adamant commands is that we've got to stop judging? That you came to call sinners, not the just? That you can never stop loving me? Keep reminding me, now and always, of what it means to follow you.

April 30: Tuesday of the Fifth Week of Easter

Under Pressure

Readings: Acts 14:19-28; John 14:27-31a

Scripture: "It is necessary for us to undergo many hardships to enter the Kingdom of God." (Acts 14:22)

Reflection: When Paul and Barnabas tell the Christian community at the end of their first missionary journey that they will have to endure hardships to enter the kingdom of God, they likely have in mind the stoning that had almost killed Paul in the neighboring city of Lystra some days earlier.

For the vast majority of us, that kind of hardship is an extremely remote possibility. That being the case, what kind of hardship might we have to undergo to enter the kingdom of God?

The Greek word *thlipsis* is often translated as persecution, affliction, or hardship, as it is in this verse. What it literally means, however, is pressure—pressure caused by problems that seem insolvable.

Meeting with families in the Philippines on January 16, 2015, Pope Francis spoke about his way of dealing with pressure: "I have great love for Saint Joseph, because he is a man of silence and strength. On my table I have an image of Saint Joseph sleeping. Even when he is asleep, he is taking care of the church! Yes! We know that he can do that. So when I have a problem, a difficulty, I write a little note and I put it underneath Saint Joseph, so that he can dream about it! In other words, I tell him: pray for this problem!"

If being part of the kingdom of God means recognizing that God is in control, that all we are and do is in the hands of God, and that the saints can help and inspire us, then the times when we feel under pressure may allow us to see that the kingdom of God is present among us.

Meditation: Think of the times in your life when you felt under pressure and didn't see any way out of it. Did you turn to God or one of the saints in prayer? Or did you perhaps think that doing so would be a sign of immaturity? Isn't it interesting that Pope Francis doesn't ask St. Joseph to take away his problem but to pray for it?

Prayer: I lie down and I fall asleep,
              [and] I will wake up, for the LORD sustains me.
           I do not fear, then, thousands of people
              arrayed against me on every side. (Ps 3:6-7)

Abide with Me

Readings: Acts 15:1-6; John 15:1-8

Scripture: "Just as a branch cannot bear fruit on its own unless it remains on the vine, so neither can you unless you remain in me." (John 15:4)

Reflection: The hymn "Abide with Me" by Henry Francis Lyte has been described as "intensely personal yet, as it has proved, wholly universal." This hymn's popularity can be seen by the fact that, according to the website Hymnary.org, it is published in 1,575 hymnals.

It appears that Lyte wrote this hymn in 1820 while visiting a dying friend who kept repeating the phrase "Abide with me." Lyte himself died twenty-seven years later at the age of fifty-four. His daughter recalled, "In the evening of the same day [when he preached his last sermon] he placed in the hands of a near and dear relative the little hymn, 'Abide with Me.'"

Although the biblical text on which the hymn is based is Luke 24:29, where the disciples invite the yet unrecognized risen Jesus to abide with them as the day draws to an end, it can also serve as a fitting meditation on the words Jesus spoke to his disciples on the night before he died: "Abide in me as I abide in you" (John 15:4, NRSV).

Jesus' promise to abide with his followers for all time is also his final message to his disciples in the Gospel of Matthew: "And behold, I am with you always, until the end of the age" (28:20).

Jesus abiding with us and we with him is the fruit of his resurrection. He is no longer bound by time and space. His abiding with us—in our minds and hearts—and our abiding with him is ultimately what makes our lives fruitful in works of justice, love, and peace.

Meditation: Lyte's hymn is a prayer that Jesus remain present with us in every trial and especially at the moment of death. If, as St. Benedict counsels, we are to keep death daily before our eyes, one way to do that is to become ever more conscious that the risen Jesus, who abides in us at every moment, will not abandon us at death.

Prayer: I fear no foe, with Thee at hand to bless; Ills have no weight, and tears no bitterness. Where is death's sting? Where, grave, thy victory? I triumph still, if Thou abide with me. (Henry Francis Lyte, "Abide with Me")

Listen!

Readings: Acts 15:7-21; John 15:9-11

Scripture: The whole assembly fell silent, and they listened . . . (Acts 15:12)

Reflection: In the first years of the Christian movement, some Jewish Christians were convinced that Gentiles had to follow the law of Moses in order to be admitted to the community of believers. "Unless you are circumcised according to the Mosaic practice," they insisted, "you cannot be saved" (Acts 15:1).

Others argued that since even Jewish Christians were saved through the grace of the Lord Jesus rather than through their observance of the law, there was no reason to require Gentiles to submit themselves to the requirements of the Mosaic law.

That particular issue is obviously not one that divides the church today, but the way the early church responded to this division of Christians into opposing camps has much to offer our contemporary church.

What is remarkable about Luke's account of the meeting that took place in Jerusalem to resolve this issue is that even though both sides were convinced they were right, at a certain point, they fell silent, and they *listened* to one another.

Imagine that!

Furthermore, they listened in an orderly and disciplined way. First, Paul and Barnabas reported on what was actually happening "out in the field"—God was already working signs and wonders among the Gentiles. Then they listened to the Scriptures as James, the leader of the Christian community in Jerusalem, showed them that the incidents Peter, Paul, and Barnabas had described to them were in line with what prophets had said in ages past.

Listening to one another and to the word of God, revealed through the Scriptures and in the lives of real people, is the way to begin healing divisions.

Meditation: Think about the people, programs, and voices in print and social media you listen to. It takes conscious effort to listen with an open mind to those we don't agree with, trying to understand why they think the way they do. But unless we make that effort, there is no real listening but only an attempt to score points for "our side."

Prayer: From presumption restrain your servant;
  may it not rule me.
  Then shall I be blameless,
  clean from grave sin.
    (Ps 19:14, Abbey Psalms and Canticles)

Seeing God

Readings: 1 Cor 15:1-8; John 14:6-14

Scripture: "Master, show us the Father, and that will be enough for us." (John 14:8)

Reflection: You may have heard the story of a kindergarten teacher whose pupils were working on a drawing assignment. As she walked around the room, she stopped by one of them and asked what he was drawing. "God," he answered. "Well, well, well," said the teacher. "But nobody knows what God looks like." Without missing a beat, the little boy replied, "They will now."

Philip has just heard Jesus say, "If you know me, then you will also know my Father. From now on you do know him and have seen him" (John 14:7). He probably cannot imagine that Jesus actually said what he thinks he heard him say and asks Jesus to show them the Father.

So Jesus speaks to Philip directly, "Have I been with you for so long a time and you still do not know me, Philip? Whoever has seen me has seen the Father" (John 14:9).

Jesus is God's "body language." Jesus does not show us what God looks like but what God does. "Seeing God" means coming to an understanding of *how* God is, of what God *does*. In other words, when you say "God," think of that word as a verb more than as a noun.

In his first letter, St. John famously says, "God is love" (1 John 4:16). Look at how Jesus "does" love. He cures. He teaches. He comforts. In doing so, he shows us the Father, who is love in action.

If we do as Jesus does, even in the smallest way, God can also be seen in us.

Meditation: If seeing Jesus means seeing God (the Father), and if being a follower of Jesus means remaining in him and he in us (see John 15:4), then it follows that doing as Jesus did, loving and forgiving as Jesus loved and forgave, is what makes God visible in our world.

Prayer: Where charity and love are, there God is. Therefore, whensoever we are gathered as one, lest we in mind be divided, let us beware. Let cease malicious quarrels, let strife give way. And in the midst of us be Christ our God. (*Ubi caritas*, hymn attributed to Paulinus of Aquileia)

May 4: Saturday of the Fifth Week of Easter

Why Do They Hate Us?

Readings: Acts 16:1-10; John 15:18-21

Scripture: "If the world hates you . . ." (John 15:18)

Reflection: "Hate" is a strong word. When Jesus uses it in other contexts—for example, when he says, "If any one comes to me without hating his father and mother, wife and children, brothers and sisters, and even his own life, he cannot be my disciple" (Luke 14:26)—we are usually pretty quick to soften his words. Rather than interpreting them as literal instructions to "hate," we interpret them as meaning that family has to take second place if we want to follow Jesus.

Perhaps a similar softening is in order when Jesus warns us of the possibility that the world will hate us because we do not belong to the world.

There certainly are cases of real hatred of Christians, a hatred that leads to violence and even slaughter. What is more common, however, is criticism of Christians for being judgmental, hypocritical, sectarian, and standoffish. The world may not so much hate us as dismiss us as irrelevant, claiming we have nothing constructive or enlightening to say with regard to the world's major challenges.

Being dismissed as irrelevant or hated for daring to question and even criticize positions and policies that we consider harmful of our well-being as a society can certainly cause us anguish. But it can also be a call to conversion, a call to be less judgmental, less confrontational in our criticism of what we believe is wrong, and more willing to admit that we might have something to learn from those we disagree with.

Meditation: Perhaps we are afraid that if we do not express our opposition to individuals or organizations that promote what we consider to be immoral or destructive behaviors, we are aiding and abetting them. What we need to consider—and perhaps change—is the way we criticize what we believe to be wrong and our tendency to rush to judgment before examining the reasons we and others believe and act in a certain way.

Prayer: Let the words of my mouth be acceptable,
              the thoughts of my heart before you,
              Lord, my rock and my redeemer. (Ps 19:15)

A Sacrifice of Love

Readings: Acts 10:25-26, 34-35, 44-48; 1 John 4:7-10; John 15:9-17

Scripture: [God] loved us and sent his Son as expiation for our sins. (1 John 4:10)

Reflection: We've gotten so used to statements such as "Jesus died for our sins and took on himself the punishment that we deserved" or "God needed a perfect sacrifice to atone for our sins and that's why Jesus had to suffer and die" that we may be surprised to learn that this way of understanding the passion and death of Jesus is shocking, even offensive, to the followers of other religious traditions.

Muslims, who reverence Jesus as a great Prophet, cannot understand why an all-merciful God needs to have Jesus suffer an ignominious death in order to win pardon for our sins.

Buddhists are also bewildered by the way Christians regard the crucifixion. The renowned Buddhist teacher Thich Nhat Hanh gently put it this way: "[The cross] is a very painful image for me. It does not convey joy or peace, and this does not do justice to Jesus."

We have to admit that regarding the death of Jesus as a way of appeasing an offended and angry God, even though it may have made sense in the feudal society of medieval Europe, is inadequate. Jesus makes clear the meaning of his passion and death when he says, "No one has greater love than this, to lay down one's life for one's friends" (John 15:13). And not just for one's friends. As Paul points out, "while we were enemies, we were reconciled to God through the death of his Son" (Rom 5:10). Jesus does not die because God is angry with us. Jesus dies because he loves his Father and us more than his own life.

Meditation: The reason the cross brings us peace and joy is that we see in it the ultimate expression of Jesus' love for sinners, not only for his executioners but for everyone who has ever hedged on the command to love God and neighbor. Recognizing this love shown in the crucifixion doesn't "get us off the hook." It is what calls us and enables us to be loving and forgiving.

Prayer: May Christ dwell in my heart through faith, that rooted and grounded in love, I may have strength to comprehend what is the breadth and length and height and depth, and to know the love of Christ that surpasses knowledge, so that I may be filled with all the fullness of God. (Adapted from Eph 3:17-19)

May 6: Monday of the Sixth Week of Easter

The Woman Who Prevailed

Readings: Acts 16:11-15; John 15:26–16:4a

Scripture: [S]he prevailed on us. (Acts 16:15)

Reflection: One word can tell us a lot about Lydia, the dealer in purple cloth from the city of Thyatira who offered hospitality to Paul and his companions.

As Luke puts it, "[S]he prevailed on us." *Prevailed* would seem to indicate that her initial invitation was declined: "Oh, we couldn't possibly impose ourselves on your generosity" or "We'd love to, but we really must be on our way. We just don't have the time to stop and rest."

You can almost hear her reply: "Nonsense. You're spending the night at my place, period." So they stayed—and later returned.

At the end of chapter 16 Luke tells us that Paul and Silas ran into opposition when they continued their preaching in Philippi and were imprisoned. But after an earthquake set them loose and the magistrates sent them on their way, they "went to Lydia's house where they saw and encouraged the brothers, and then they left" (Acts 16:40).

Lydia's house, it appears, had become a center for the Christian community. The businesswoman from Thyatira joined the ranks of women converts who became leaders of

Christian communities that formed in response to Paul's preaching.

Passages from Paul's letters about wives being subject to their husbands (Eph 5:22) or women keeping silent in church (1 Cor 14:24) are sometimes used to argue that women are ineligible for leadership in Christian communities. A closer reading of the Scriptures, however, makes it pretty clear that this was not Paul's position.

Meditation: Reflect on the many ways women, by their courageous and devoted lives of prayer, service, leadership, and love, have built up the church from the time of Jesus and Paul to the present day. Have you known some of these women in your own family or parish community?

Prayer: We give you thanks, Lord, for the many women who have prevailed. Continue to strengthen the hope of both women and men for a church that will fully recognize and welcome the gifts of women, as did Jesus and the early Christian communities.

May 7: Tuesday of the Sixth Week of Easter

When Leaving Is Better

Readings: Acts 16:22-34; John 16:5-11

Scripture: "[I]t is better for you that I go." (John 16:7)

Reflection: In one of her most poignant poems, a grief-stricken Emily Dickinson wrote,

> My life closed twice before its close—
> It yet remains to see
> If Immortality unveil
> A third event to me

> So huge, so hopeless to conceive
> As these that twice befell.
> Parting is all we know of heaven,
> And all we need of hell.

We all know how painful parting can be, whether caused by death, divorce, the breaking up of a friendship, or moving to another location. And yet, Jesus says, "It is better for you that I go."

One way to understand this puzzling statement is given by Carlo Carretto, a twentieth-century Italian spiritual writer. "I was thirsty for presence," he writes, "so, in order to stretch out my desire, [Jesus] presented Himself as absence. Therefore, I was obliged to purify my faith and tell Him I believed in Him, not out of self-interest, but out of love." Feeling and enjoying the presence of Jesus in our lives can make us self-satisfied; feeling his absence may be what we need to learn to turn to him not for what we can gain, but simply in order to love him.

Jesus offers an even deeper reason for his going. He does not want to part from us; he wants to abide with us. But he does not want to be with us simply by being alongside us; he does not want us to keep clinging to him, as he said to Mary Magdalene, who recognized and embraced him after his resurrection (John 20:17). Rather, Jesus' greatest desire is to dwell within us.

Christ lives in us by sending his Spirit to us. It is thanks to that Holy Spirit, our Advocate, that we can say with the apostle Paul, "[I]t is no longer I who live, but it is Christ who lives in me" (Gal 2:20, NRSV).

Meditation: Our lives are filled with partings—some ordinary and daily, others painful and overwhelming. Ponder some of the partings that have marked your life, how you dealt with them, and what you learned from them.

Prayer: Lord Jesus, in those times when I feel nothing but your absence in my life, help me to understand that you are making my desire for you grow stronger so I may see you more clearly, love you more dearly, and follow you more nearly, day by day.

Seeking, Feeling, Finding God

Readings: Acts 17:15, 22–18:1; John 16:12-15

Scripture: . . . that people might seek God, even perhaps grope for him and find him . . . (Acts 17:27)

Reflection: Luke gives us a summary of Paul's speech to the Athenians, but even an abridged version reveals what a rhetorical gem it is.

Paul begins by winning over his audience. He notes the abundance of altars in the city and, rather than criticizing their polytheism, he compliments his hearers on being so religious. Paul then helps the Athenians recognize that there is one God who is the source of all that is, whose life-giving breath unifies the human race, and whose ordering of seasons and boundaries leads human beings to "seek God, even perhaps grope for him and find him."

"Seek, grope, and find" is a marvelous summary of our way to faith (provided we don't get hung up on the word "grope," which is a rather strange way of translating the Greek verb meaning "to feel, to verify by contact"). The first step of faith is seeking, asking what or who could be responsible for the incredible order and beauty we find in our world. Seeking leads us to feeling, in our bodies as much as in our minds, the presence of "someone" who is responsible for all this order and beauty. And then, through God's gracious self-revelation, above all in the person of Jesus, we find the God in whom "we live and move and have our being" (Acts 17:28).

Paul's assertion that God raised this Jesus from the dead was too much for most of Paul's audience to accept, but some in that Athenian crowd embraced it—as do we, who see in the risen Jesus God's way to us and our way to God.

Meditation: At some time or other, we have probably all "groped" for God, wondering why God felt so distant, or asking how an all-loving and all-powerful God allowed something terrible to happen. Has there also been a time when such searching led you to a sense that God was within you, not to explain why something bad happened, but to comfort, console, and strengthen you?

Prayer: Dear Lord, I know that feeling the joy of your presence in my life is not necessary for me to have faith that you are always with me—but it sure helps.

May 9: Thursday of the Sixth Week of Easter
(or The Ascension of the Lord)

Today's Aquilas and Priscillas

Readings: Acts 18:1-8; John 16:16-20 (or Acts 1:1-11; Eph 1:17-23 or 4:1-13 or 4:1-7, 11-13; Mark 16:15-20)

Scripture: [In Corinth Paul] met a Jew named Aquila . . . who had recently come from Italy with his wife Priscilla because Claudius had ordered all the Jews to leave Rome. (Acts 18:2)

Reflection: The Roman historian Suetonius tells us that the emperor Claudius "banished from Rome all the Jews, who were continually making disturbances at the instigation of one Chrestus." This likely means that this particular expulsion of the Jews was not an expression of the anti-Semitism that later spawned innumerable pogroms and most horrendously the Holocaust (*Shoah*)—persecutions that often took place at the instigation and with the participation of many who called themselves Christians. Rather, it was likely decreed to put an end to civil unrest within the Jewish community caused by conflicting views regarding Jesus.

Claudius's decree is usually dated to the year 49, so it is likely that by that time a good number of Jews living in Rome believed that Jesus was the Messiah. Aquila and Priscilla had probably endeavored to persuade their fellow Jews to share their faith in Jesus.

The ministry of Aquila and Priscilla is yet another indication that laymen and women were at the very center of establishing, forming, and caring for the first Christian communities. The growing number of Aquilas and Priscillas in our parishes—laypeople with great capacity for evangelizing and building up the church—can surely be regarded as a sign that the Spirit is at work in the church today, raising up varieties of gifts, services, and activities, all of them activated "by one and the same Spirit, who allots to each one individually just as the Spirit chooses" (1 Cor 12:11, NRSV).

Meditation: The Christian community in Rome to whom Paul wrote his longest and most influential letter was probably not large. Yet at the end of his letter, he greets about thirty individuals and families, including Priscilla and Aquila, referring to many of them as "workers in the Lord" (Rom 16:12). We speak of ourselves as "members" of a parish. What might our parishes be like if we described ourselves as "workers," all of whom contribute in their own unique way to building up a community of worship and service?

Prayer: Servants of the Lord, bless the Lord;
praise and exalt him above all forever.
Spirits and souls of the just, bless the Lord;
praise and exalt him above all forever.
Holy and humble of heart, bless the Lord;
praise and exalt him above all forever.
(Dan 3:85-87)

Praying in Jesus' Name

Readings: Acts 18:9-18; John 16:20-23

Scripture: "[W]hatever you ask the Father in my name he will give you." (John 16:23)

Reflection: Who among us has not been disappointed, even crushed, when we didn't receive what we fervently prayed for? A sick friend did not recover; we didn't get the grade we needed to be accepted by the college we had our heart set on; the biopsy revealed that the tumor was cancerous.

Could it be that we do not receive what we ask for because, as the apostle James tells us, we "ask wrongly, to spend it on [our] passions" (Jas 4:3)?

Admittedly, those are strong, even harsh, words. To "spend on our passions" literally means, "to squander what we receive in luxurious indulgence." That might be true if we are praying to win the Powerball lottery, but hardly when our prayer is for the recovery of someone who is gravely ill.

But James's explanation of why our prayers are not answered—that is, not answered in the way we want them to be—can be interpreted as a clarification of what Jesus meant when he said that whatever we asked for in his name would be given by the Father. Since the name "Jesus" means "God saves (rescues, delivers, heals)," one way to understand what asking for something in Jesus' name means is that we want

God to grant what will be most beneficial for us or for the one we are praying for—what is most saving or healing for us—and leave it up to God to determine what that is.

Ultimately, prayer in Jesus' name means praying as he taught us and as he himself prayed to the Father: "[Y]our will be done, / on earth as in heaven" (Matt 6:10) and "[N] ot my will but yours be done" (Luke 22:42).

Meditation: As an old saying has it, "Be careful what you pray for. You might get it." Sometimes what we think is best for us really isn't what is best. On the other hand, God might give us exactly what we prayed for in order to show us it's not at all what we needed. In the end, the more we can imitate Jesus and surrender our own will to God's will, the better off we will be.

Prayer: Pray the Our Father, with special attention to the third petition: Thy will be done, on earth as it is in heaven.

May 11: Saturday of the Sixth Week of Easter

Accurate and More Accurate

Readings: Acts 18:23-28; John 16:23b-28

Scripture: [Apollos] spoke and taught accurately about Jesus. . . . Priscilla and Aquila . . . took him aside and explained to him the Way of God more accurately. (Acts 18:25-26)

Reflection: Luke tells us that an eloquent speaker from Alexandria by the name of Apollos was instructed in the "Way of the Lord," and that he accurately taught things about Jesus. Luke goes on to say that when Priscilla and Aquila heard him, they took him aside and explained to him the "Way of God." That contrast between the "Way of the Lord" and the "Way of God" may be the key to understanding what is going on here.

Apollos probably regarded Jesus as a great teacher, a great model for life. As Luke says, having been instructed in the "Way of the Lord" ("Lord" being a title for Jesus), he spoke "accurately" about Jesus. However, he may not yet have come to recognize in Jesus the glory of God manifested in human flesh. For that reason, Priscilla and Aquila took it upon themselves to explain to him the "Way of God" more accurately.

Jesus is more than just a teacher. Jesus—through his life, death, and resurrection—*reveals God*. In Jesus we see the

Father, through Jesus we are drawn close to God. In his body broken for us, his blood poured out for us, the infinitely generous love of God is made visible in our world.

Meditation: We often think of Jesus in terms of his teaching and the many examples of love and compassion he gives, all of which are good and true. What we may need to be more attentive to is that Jesus doesn't just tell us what to do. His words and deeds reveal what God is doing—doing in us, for us, and through us.

Prayer: Lord Jesus, I confess that I often do not see what you are doing in me and for me. Open my eyes so that I do not miss the "mustard seeds" of generosity, kindness, and joyful self-giving that surround me and are signs of you and your kingdom.

May 12: The Ascension of the Lord
(or Seventh Sunday of Easter)

Heaven Is Here

Readings: Acts 1:1-11; Eph 1:17-23 or 4:1-13 or 4:1-7, 11-13; Mark 16:15-20 (or Acts 1:15-17, 20a, 20c-26; 1 John 4:11-16; John 17:11b-19)

Scripture: [Jesus] was lifted up, and a cloud took him from their sight. (Acts 1:9)

Reflection: The feast of the Ascension provides an occasion to reflect a bit on our understanding of heaven. What are Mark and Luke trying to tell us when they say that Jesus was "lifted up" (Acts 1:9) or "taken up into heaven" (Mark 16:19)?

To even begin to answer that question, we have to recognize that when we speak of heaven we are dealing with a different kind of reality, one for which our common categories of space or matter or even time simply do not apply.

According to the eminent biblical scholar N. T. Wright, heaven and earth are "two different dimensions of God's good creation. And the point about heaven is twofold. First, heaven relates to earth tangentially so that the one who is in heaven can be present simultaneously anywhere and everywhere on earth; the ascension therefore means that Jesus is available, accessible, without people having to travel to a particular spot on the earth to find him."

Jesus has ascended to heaven and is seated at God's right hand, and yet he is with us. What this tells us is that God's space and our space—heaven and earth, in other words—are very different, and yet not far away from one another at all. In fact, they intersect.

Heaven is not a faraway place, not some kind of strictly spiritual place to which Jesus ascended and our souls go when we die. It's God's space, even here on earth, a space in which Jesus dwells both spiritually and bodily. And when we enter into this space, we will find that it's very much like the space we are in now, only much more solid, much brighter, much sharper than anything we have ever seen or experienced before.

We might even say it will be heaven on earth.

Meditation: How do you think about or picture heaven? How might you have experienced at some point in your life the "intersection" of heaven and earth? Have you ever thought of heaven not so much as a place but as the fullness of life that can be ours?

Prayer: Heavenly Father, eye has not seen, ear has not heard, nor can we even imagine the joy you have prepared for us. Make strong our hope that we will behold the fullness of your splendor—and of ours—when we depart this temporary dwelling and enter the one you have prepared for us from and for all eternity.

Cheer Up!

Readings: Acts 19:1-8; John 16:29-33

Scripture: "[T]ake courage, I have conquered the world." (John 16:33)

Reflection: There is a word in today's Gospel that only occurs eight times in the New Testament. It is always given as an instruction or command and, with one exception, is only spoken by Jesus. That word—*thaseō*—is often translated as "Take courage." But it also means "Be of good cheer" or, more colloquially, "Cheer up."

Jesus tells the paralyzed man to cheer up because his sins have been forgiven.

He tells the woman who had suffered from hemorrhages for twelve years to cheer up because her faith has made her well.

He tells his terrified disciples who think they are seeing a ghost walking on the water to cheer up and not be afraid because he is with them.

Bartimaeus, who is blind, is told to cheer up because Jesus is calling him.

Jesus appears to Paul in prison and tells him to cheer up because he will also bear witness in Rome.

Today he tells us to cheer up because he has overcome the world.

Our natural tendency is to see all the things that are going wrong, all the failures, all the evidence of sin in the world and in our lives. But that's not the whole story. In fact, it's little more than a sideshow. The real story is that God's love, poured into our hearts by the Spirit through the life, death, resurrection, and ascension of Jesus, is stronger than sickness, fear, and sin—is stronger than the world.

So, cheer up!

Meditation: "Cheer up" is the last thing we would want to say to someone who is in anguish. However, on some occasions it may be what we need to say to ourselves. We can only do that if we remember how we have been comforted and supported in the past and pray that we will again come to know the power of God's love in our lives, a love often shown through the kindness of friends, families, and even strangers.

Prayer: But here I am miserable and in pain;
            let your saving help protect me, God,
        That I may praise God's name in song
            and glorify it with thanksgiving. . . .
        "See, you lowly ones, and be glad;
            you who seek God, take heart!"
            (Ps 69:30-31, 33)

The Church's First Mistake?

Readings: Acts 1:15-17, 20-26; John 15:9-17

Scripture: [T]he lot fell upon Matthias . . . (Acts 1:26)

Reflection: Could it be that the choice of Matthias to replace Judas was the church's first mistake? The reason some have suggested this possibility is that after Matthias was chosen, the Scriptures never speak of him again. Perhaps God already had someone else in mind—someone whose name was Saul (also known as Paul), the Pharisee who became an apostle.

Whether it was a mistake or not, the decision to fill the position left vacant by the death of Judas was made in haste. Jesus had instructed his followers to wait for the coming of the Holy Spirit (Acts 1:4-5), but Peter jumped the gun. Right after the ascension, he told the believers that they were the ones who had to fulfill the Scriptures by appointing someone to take the place of Judas. So they nominated two and then prayed that the Lord would show them whom he had chosen. But the fact is, they had already decided that it would be one of the two they had nominated. Casting lots was, in effect, a way to coerce the Lord into confirming the choice they had made.

There are times when immediate action is called for, but acting in haste is generally not a good idea. Sometimes we need to slow down in order to gather more information and, above all, give ourselves time to recognize what God is asking us to do—or accept.

In those situations when immediate action is not necessary, we can wait in confidence because, as the Brazilians put it, *"Deus tarda mas não falha."* God delays but never fails.

Meditation: It may seem shocking to speak about the church making a mistake, especially right at the beginning of its existence. Jesus never promised that the church built on Peter would never make a mistake, but that the gates of hell would "not prevail against it" (Matt 16:18). What is important is what the church can learn from its mistakes—and we from ours—and what needs to be done so they will not be repeated.

Prayer: Give me the grace, O Lord, to say "I was wrong" when I make a mistake, as I often will.

Dress the Part

Readings: Acts 20:28-38; John 17:11b-19

Scripture: "I have never wanted anyone's silver or gold or clothing." (Acts 20:33)

Reflection: Scriptural references to clothing often highlight its symbolic meaning. For example, the father of the prodigal son ordered that his son be clothed with the "finest robe" when he returned from his wandering, a sign of the father's extravagant love and forgiveness (Luke 15:22). The towel or apron Jesus put on when he washed the disciples' feet—and then doesn't take off—emphasizes his role as servant (John 13:4). The seamless garment he was stripped of before being nailed to the cross symbolizes that Jesus died "to gather into one the dispersed children of God" (John 11:52).

When Paul said he never wanted anyone's clothing, could he have been thinking of its symbolic meaning? He wasn't going to dress as a polished Greek orator, seeking to sway people with fancy rhetoric and subtle logic. Nor was he going to dress like a learned scholar of Jewish law, even though he was a brilliant Pharisee. He was going to appear in the work clothes he wore when making tents to show that the Good News of what God accomplished in Jesus, crucified and risen, was for all people, ordinary people, working people like himself.

Scripture also uses clothing as a symbol of our life in Christ. As Bishop Erik Varden of Trondheim, Norway, once put it in his blog *Coram Fratribus,* "When Paul speaks of 'putting on the Lord Jesus Christ,' the reference is not to some kind of loose poncho that fits on top of various layers of other personally chosen garments. To be a Christian is to be transformed. We must shed the old outfit."

Meditation: Why do we dress the way we do? To let others know the kind of person we are, or the kind of person we want them to think we are, or the kind of person we aspire to be? Does our faith have anything to do with our choices? Should it?

Prayer: I will rejoice heartily in the LORD,
            my being exults in my God;
        For he has clothed me with garments of salvation,
            and wrapped me in a robe of justice. (Isa 61:10)

Two Little Words

Readings: Acts 22:30; 23:6-11; John 17:20-26

Scripture: "[T]hat they may all be one, as you, Father, are in me and I in you, that they also may be in us . . ." (John 17:21)

Reflection: In the Nicene Creed we profess that Jesus is "consubstantial with the Father." The word "consubstantial" translates *homoousios*, the Greek word used at the Council of Nicaea in the year 325 to affirm that God the Son and God the Father are of the "same substance." The council thereby rejected the position that Jesus was of a "similar substance" (*homoiousios*) to that of God the Father. That decision led some wags to observe that whether or not you were a heretic depended on a single letter of the alphabet!

In every language, single letters and tiny words can make a great difference. For that reason, it's important to look carefully at what Jesus means when he says, "[A]s you, Father, are *in* me and I *in* you, that they also may be *in* us" (John 17:21).

When Jesus says that he is *in* the Father and the Father *in* him, he means that his will is one with the Father's will. We see this when Jesus prays on the night before he died, "Father, if you are willing, take this cup away from me; still, not my will but yours be done" (Luke 22:42).

In his Rule, St. Benedict captures beautifully what it means to be one *as* Jesus and God the Father are one. Monks are to show good zeal by "supporting with the greatest patience one another's weaknesses of body or behavior. . . . No one is to pursue what he judges better for himself, but instead, what he judges better for someone else" (RB 72.5-7).

Aspiring to that kind of good zeal is what makes for unity and peace in families as well as in monasteries.

Meditation: Pursuing what is better for someone else rather than for oneself could almost be a definition of what it means to be a parent. Can you think of occasions apart from your family when you consciously chose what was better for another rather than for yourself? Have there been times when it has been difficult to discern what was truly best for another person? How might you handle these situations?

Prayer: How very good and pleasant it is
                    when kindred live together in unity! . . .
              It is like the dew of Hermon,
                    which falls on the mountains of Zion.
              For there the LORD ordained his blessing,
                    life forevermore. (Ps 133, NRSV)

With Us in Times of Trouble

Readings: Acts 25:13b-21; John 21:15-19

Scripture: "[W]hen you grow old, you will stretch out your hands, and someone else will dress you and lead you where you do not want to go." (John 21:18)

Reflection: "No good deed goes unpunished." That humorous but cynical observation could well be a commentary on the words of Jesus to Peter in today's Gospel.

Peter had, in fact, done something really good. By his triple profession of love for Jesus, he acknowledged his triple denial of Jesus and sought forgiveness. But rather than praising Peter for his love and repentance, Jesus speaks to him about the suffering and death that await him.

It's almost second nature to think that if we do something good, things will work out well for us, and if we do something bad, misfortune will befall us. That may be true in the long run, but it is certainly not always the case as we live our lives. The book of Job makes that very clear. Even those who have never done anything wrong can experience unspeakable hardship and suffering. When Job demands that God explain this seemingly terrible injustice, the only response he gets is essentially: "My ways are mysterious; who are you to question me?"

Jesus Christ does not explain the mystery of God's ways. Rather, he offers us the good news that he is Emmanuel, God with us. Pain and loss are an unavoidable part of human life, even for those who are good, but Jesus promises to stay with us even when we are being led where we do not want to go.

The unconditional love of God—given a human face in Jesus and poured into our hearts through the Holy Spirit—is what strengthens us in adversity, consoles us in sorrow, and keeps hope burning in our hearts even when everything seems to be slipping away.

Meditation: When we say that the love of God strengthens us, consoles us, and gives us hope, we can remember that God's love is usually shown through other people. When someone you know is suffering in body or spirit and bears the additional pain of thinking that their suffering is meaningless, how might you strengthen and console them?

Prayer: Blessed be the God and Father of our Lord Jesus Christ, the Father of compassion and God of all encouragement. (2 Cor 1:3)

Who Are We to Judge?

Readings: Acts 28:16-20, 30-31; John 21:20-25

Scripture: "What concern is it of yours? You follow me." (John 21:22)

Reflection: Back in the day, when I was a novice, one of our tasks was to walk through the monastery each morning at 4:30, ringing a bell to call the monks to prayer. On my rounds I would pass the room of a monk who had taped to the door frame of his room a small card on which he had written the words of Jesus to Peter in Latin: "*Quid ad te? Tu sequere me.*" This translates to: "What concern is it of yours? You follow me" (John 21:22). Each time he went in or out of his room, this monk was reminded of his vocation to seek God and not wonder about what his brothers were up to—or worse, pass judgment on them.

The seasons of Lent and Easter invite us to become more intentional about deepening our faith and growing in virtue. That high and noble endeavor also carries with it the danger of patting ourselves on the back for the progress we have made and looking down our noses at those whom we judge as not nearly as devout or virtuous as we are.

To follow Christ raised from the dead means dying to ourselves and being raised with him, emptying ourselves of the false ego that constantly clamors for attention and judges others to be less observant, less virtuous, less holy than we are.

We easily forget that one of the clearest signs that the risen Christ dwells in us and we in him is that we are becoming less judgmental and more loving. That is what it means to be an Easter people.

Meditation: It is, of course, good to be interested in others—what they are doing, what they are thinking—and to offer, as appropriate, encouragement or counsel. The problem lies in constantly comparing ourselves to others and then either belittling them or ourselves. If we focus our attention on what we need to do to follow Christ more closely, we will be much less likely either to pat ourselves on the back or to be critical of others.

Prayer: Save me, Lord, from comparing myself to others, whether I am reinforcing my sense of superiority or putting myself down. Keep me from presuming that I know what motivates others to do what they do. Show me all the ways you are calling me to experience the joy of giving myself unselfishly, and that will be enough.

May 19: Pentecost Sunday

The Breath of God

Readings: Acts 2:1-11; 1 Cor 12:3b-7, 12-13 or Gal 5:16-25; John 20:19-23 or 15:26-27; 16:12-15

Scripture: [Jesus] breathed on them and said to them, "Receive the Holy Spirit." (John 20:22)

Reflection: On the day of his resurrection, Jesus does what God did when Adam was created.

God breathed into a human body, made from the dust of the ground, and a "living being" came into existence (Gen 2:7).

Jesus breathes on his disciples, and the church, the Body of the risen Lord, comes into existence.

On Pentecost, fifty days later, the Holy Spirit descends on those same disciples with a sound "like a strong driving wind," enabling them to proclaim the Good News.

God is breath, wind, spirit. Breath, however, may be the most compelling way of speaking of the ultimately unknowable One who spoke to Moses from a burning bush and whose name in Hebrew is written יהוה (written and read from right to left; the letters are *yod he vav he*). These letters are usually transliterated into English as YHWH. When joined to vowels, the name God revealed to Moses can be pronounced "Yahweh." It is usually interpreted to mean something like "the One who is" (cf. Exod 3:14).

104 *Pentecost Sunday*

Another explanation of the meaning of these consonants comes from the way they would sound by themselves—perhaps something like the sound of inhaling and exhaling. God's name, in other words, might simply be the sound of breathing.

God is the Breath of Life. God is the Breathing Spirit of the World. We say, "I breathe," but it might be more accurate to say "I am breathed" or "My breath is God breathing in me."

Breathing is really not something we do; it is something that happens of itself, usually without our being conscious of it. In a similar way, we are in God and God in us even when we don't notice it or think about it.

How great is that!

Meditation: Today's feast of the outpouring of the Holy Spirit on Pentecost brings to completion the great fifty-day celebration of Easter. This is a time for giving thanks for all that God has done and continues to do to bring everything created to the fullness of life.

Prayer: Breathe on me, Breath of God, fill me with life anew, that I may love the way you love, and do what you would do. (Edwin Hatch, "Breathe on Me, Breath of God")

References

Introduction
Pope John Paul II, Apostolic Journey to the Far East and Oceania, Angelus, Adelaide, Australia, November 30, 1986, https://www.vatican.va/content/john-paul-ii/en/angelus/1986/documents/hf_jp-ii_ang_19861130.pdf.

April 7: Second Sunday of Easter
Pope Francis, Pastoral Visit to Genoa, Meeting with the Youth of the Diocese, May 27, 2017. (Translation from Italian: *"Amare. Amare è avere la capacità di stringere la mano sporca e la capacità di guardare gli occhi di quelli che sono in situazione di degrado e dire: 'Per me, tu sei Gesù.'"*)

April 10: Wednesday of the Second Week of Easter
Stephen G. Adubato, " 'Nobody Flees from Love': Brazil's Alternative Prisons Offer a Model of Restorative Justice," *America* (December 2021).

April 12: Friday of the Second Week of Easter
Raymond E. Brown, *A Once-and-Coming Spirit at Pentecost* (Collegeville, MN: Liturgical Press, 1994), 36.

April 17: Wednesday of the Third Week of Easter
Francis Thompson, "The Hound of Heaven." Text and recordings widely accessible online.

April 22: Monday of the Fourth Week of Easter
Louise Penny, *A Great Reckoning* (New York: Minotaur Books, 2016), 341.

May 1: Wednesday of the Fifth Week of Easter
Erik Routley, *A Panorama of Christian Hymnody* (Collegeville, MN: Liturgical Press, 1979), 45.
Frank Kidson, "Church and Organ Music: 'Abide with Me,'" *The Musical Times* (January 1, 1908): 25.

May 2: Saint Athanasius
Monks of Conception Abbey, *The Abbey Psalms and Canticles* (Washington, DC: United States Conference of Catholic Bishops, 2018).

May 5: Sixth Sunday of Easter
Catherine Corneille, ed., *Atonement and Comparative Theology* (New York: Fordham University Press, 2021), 223, 262.

May 7: Tuesday of the Sixth Week of Easter
Emily Dickinson, "My Life Closed Twice Before Its Close (96)," *Poems by Emily Dickinson* (1896), https://poets.org/poem/my-life-closed-twice-its-close-96.
Carlo Carretto, *The God Who Comes* (Maryknoll, NY: Orbis Books, 1974), 99.

May 9: Thursday of the Sixth Week of Easter
Suetonius, *Life of Claudius*, 25, https://sourcebooks.fordham.edu/ancient/suetonius-claudius-worthington.asp, cited in

Luke Timothy Johnson, *The Acts of the Apostles*, Sacra Pagina series, vol. 5 (Collegeville, MN: Liturgical Press, 1992), 325.

May 12: The Ascension of the Lord
N. T. Wright, *Surprised by Hope: Rethinking Heaven, the Resurrection, and the Mission of the Church* (San Francisco: HarperOne, 2008), 111.

May 15: Wednesday of the Seventh Week of Easter
Bishop Erik Varden, OSCO, blog entry for October 16, 2022, https://coramfratribus.com/notebook/.

May 16: Thursday of the Seventh Week of Easter
Timothy Fry, OSB, ed., *The Rule of Saint Benedict 1980* (Collegeville, MN: Liturgical Press, 1981), 295.

May 19: Pentecost Sunday
Rabbi Arthur Waskow, "Abraham's Journey in the Bible and the Jewish Midrash," in Joan Chittister, OSB, Murshid Saadi Shakur Chishti, and Rabbi Arthur Waskow, *The Tent of Abraham* (Boston: Beacon Press, 2006), 5–6.